Praise for Connections Between Us

Wow. I must say at first reading I put this book down twice and contemplated the words. As I finished my third reading it made me truly understand. This is truly a remarkable piece of poetry in motion. Beginning with the title of the book to the very last poem. Andrea you really took me on a ride. Full emotions and love. As a reader I was able to picture myself through out your work. Masterful job. I salute you and admire your courage. Great job!

— Quinton Ford
Producer: Let's Talk Radio

Andrea Lee's poetry collection *Connections Between Us* aims to do just that, make connections by delivering real, raw, emotional experiences of life. Intermingling self-love and romantic relationship intricacies, this collection is not afraid to go into those vulnerable places and reclaim power by saying what must be said. "Your manuscript could heal a soul/ with a familiar tone your voice speaks/ relatable truths…" So much in this book is relatable from betrayal to seduction. Andrea uses language to penetrate the veil of pretension and allow us to "taste the nectar of (her) thoughts" through interesting and vivid metaphors.

— James Coats
Author of *Midnight and Mad Dreams*
CLI Alumni/ Teacher

Mrs. Lee's poems are full of emotion, not only in images but in the message, she gives the readers. Even though her images are familiar and in settings we know, the profound vulnerability that the poems bring forth are powerful and raw. At a certain point the poems became the story of a life the reader knows and even though it is hard to keep reading the reader finds the courage necessary in the same poems to finish the story. Those life lessons are hard to come by and Mrs. Lee makes sure to bring those into our attention. Do not be fool by the particularly easy language found I these poems, they always say more than they show, they always show us that there is always more than meets the eye. She challenges us to become what we will by loving not by hating. A powerful collection of love, compassion and a journey we all need to take to learn again to be kind to each other.

— Maria Duarte
Editor
CLI Alumni

Andrea Lee's intimate, honest & robust collection, *Connections Between Us*, is dipped in truth, honesty & courage we all need to digest in order to embrace our authentic selves. Through the medium of poetic verses and sensual stanzas, Andrea Lee reminds us that we are worthy of being heard no matter our truth that beats in our heart. *Connections Between Us* is a classic collection, meant to be a household name. The words written purposefully on these pages are built on the divine feminine glow, and audacity to flaunt the curves of our life story. Through messages of love, intimacy, connection & the thread between us all, Lee reminds us that all we have to do is channel our experiences through our sacred pen, for these pages become more and more difficult to put down through every page. Perhaps this is simply because the connection between reader and author blooms taller and higher through every breath, sewed into the sanctuary of Lee's poems.

— RAVINA
Author of *Yellow*

Author Andrea Lee's engaging, evocative, and expressive poetry collection *Connections Between Us* is sure to captivate its readers in the first few lines of each poem! Specifically, the descriptive words are bound to magnetically draw one in to create a fantasy of their own and allow their imagination to run free. It's saucy, seductive, and sensual — and describes the highs, lows, and complexities of interpersonal relationships. This explosive book of poetry is guaranteed to take you on an emotional roller coaster while embracing the ideal of love and the deep connections between human relationships.

— Lynette E. Smith
Creator of: The Love on H.E.R Project
Counselor and Life Coach

Connections Between Us is a self-help book of poetry that will narrate you on your journey to self! Andrea Lee carefully crafted curriculum will "Plug Me In The Eclectic Symmetry that had me Levitating Above Water in my True Confessions That Forever Vibrant Discovery of We Made It" Thank you for sharing with me.

— AKoldPiece OfWork
Author of *The Weather Report*
CLI Board Of Directors President

What does it mean to respect our partnerships? How can we wholly love ourselves? How do we embrace our imperfect past and still find the courage to love again? *Connections Between Us* is a meditation on love that answers these questions with genuine grace and honest tenderness. Andrea Lee's poetry braves the bold, the broken, and the beautiful of life as each poem illuminates the waiting wisdom pulsing through the darkness of heartache and injustice. *Connections Between Us* explores the sacred spectrum of relationships from trauma bonding to divine sensuality to the liberated self. Lee's waltz with words welcomes us back home to honor our body, mind, soul and that one of a kind, precious heart.

— Alex Petunia
Author of *Tending My Wild*
CLI Faculty

In her book, *Connections Between Us*, Author A. Lee takes you on a passionate journey of love, pain, loss, and re discovery of all which encompasses the world of a woman in the struggle of everyday life. In this marvelous mixture of words and sentiments A. Lee provides the poetic foundation towards the road of self healing and self love.

— Carlos Ornelas
Author of *Ketchup: Sopa De Gato*

Andrea Lee is a poet dedicated to the craft of verse, and dedicated to the community of poets we have cultivated here at CLI. *Connections Between Us* is a powerful collection of poems exploring intimacy, love, trauma and self determination. One of poetry's great powers lies in its ability to communicate the humanity of the author's experience and observation. These poems are evidence of a life lived well, and a book well written. It is my hope that these poems make their way into the hands of the people who need them, and who might be inspired to examine themselves, and the world around them, through lyric and connection.

— Hiram Sims
Professor
"Captain" Community Literature Initiative (CLI)

Connections
between us

Connections
between us

poetry by
A. LEE

Connections Between Us
© 2023 A. Lee
ISBN: 978-1-961523-00-5

First Edition, 2023

Printed in the United States of America

Cover Artwork & Design by Starvos Pierce
Interior Artwork by Starvos Pierce
Interior Layout Design by Jim Dodson

This divine project is dedicated to all my friends, and family for all their support. They inspired me to continue my dream. So many of them have helped me and never gave up on me when I was in dire need. May God bless ALL of you always.

To all who participated in our programs, you're the reason behind the success of the events.

This book is also dedicated to all my readers. I hope that whoever finds difficulty in loving themselves first will find assistance in this book in their quest for self-love. I would love nothing more than to see you use this book as a stepping stone to start your love journey.

This book is a great testament to my growth, appreciation, and support of the great work and leadership of many who have inspired me.

And especially, to my children William, Andre, Ashlee, Alvin, and my granddaughter Audree, Ms. Bobbie Monger, Ms. LeAndrea M. Wilson, Ms. Jacqueline Ellis Trice, and Rayanna Gaines. You all are such an inspiration, and great role models, and have helped me tremendously. Much Love & Respect to you all...

Take your time, practice the steps, find yourself, and love yourself...

Acknowledgments

I would like to acknowledge all the extraordinary writers, poets, and spoken word artists in our season 10 CLI Alumni chapter: Hiram, James, Kimiko, Tami, Ja'Net, Shaquan. Thanks to Aujrel, Different Taste of Soul, Queen Quanni — we are a force to be reckoned with, and last but not least Q the producer of Let's Talk radio who also produces The Artists Connection. Q even though you're not a poet you bring so much to the poetry community. And much thanks to AJ Wone for bringing much needed value to the platform. Alex Petunia, Jasmine Banks, Maria Duarte, Lynnette Smith, Stacie Gaines, Timothey Akens, and Dolla Jonhson' Akens — indeed, you people are wonderful and I really have been honored to share this amazing journey with you. More importantly, I appreciate all the critiques on my writing and for lending a listening ear and taking the time to give me suggestions, positive praise, motivation, and encouragement; all of you are great writers. And your contributions have shown me that you all will be great authors; I look forward to reading and purchasing all of your work moving forward as you join the poetry family. Once again, thank you!

LeAndrea Wilson
There is not enough gratitude used in this lifetime that I can give you because from day one you have been a great person to me; you have been my support system, my rock, and a sister. Frankly speaking, you always show up whenever I need you without question in the 10+ years that we've been friends; we have never argued or fallen out or turned away from each other for anything or anyone and I truly appreciate that you are wise beyond your years. Love ya girl.

Stacie Gaines
Having a friend that you can call and talk with about anything, pray with and confide in is rare. From Day one when I met you welcomed me with open arms. Thank you for always including me in the important moments of your life and supporting all of my dreams. You are always just a phone call away whenever I need you. Love you girl.

Rayana Gaines
You are one of the realist, open and honest individuals I know. I appreciate your inviting beautiful spirit. You have always been a listening ear and give great positive feedback. You have always been there for me from day one — assisting me in working on my business. I appreciate all of the thoughtful greeting cards. Support is everything. Love ya girl.

Lynnette Smith

You are the epitome of excellence in everything you do. You have overcome so much in your life and still stand strong. Your encouragement and ability to make others feel seen is remarkable. Super mom always showing up and keeping your word is a great trait to have. I am honored to call you friend. You have prayed with me through many difficult situations and we made it over whatever hurdle that came our way. I wish you all the success you desire — continue to stay true to you. Love you girl.

Ravina Wadhwani

From the first moment I met you at USC season seven, your words spoke volumes you are an inspiration to many. Your words resonate across many different races of people. It's not an exaggeration that you make a connection with everyone you come in contact with and they have you as a teacher. Without mincing words, season nine has been extraordinary; I have learned so much from you and I truly appreciate everything that you bring to the table. I just want to say thank you for all the extra efforts you made to help us grow and the challenges you encouraged us to face which helped us become better writers, and also get over stage fright. In fact, you are not only a teacher, but you are a friend and authority all rolled into one person. I will always be grateful to you for your support and kindness. Love ya girl.

Alex Petunia

There are so many things that I have to say that may not fit on this page but here we go. Alex from day one when we met at USC CLI Season 7 you were welcoming. You have this magnetic spirit of love and acceptance. When you read your words from your page it is a peaceful inviting experience. I appreciate how you welcome poets from many backgrounds and cultures into your space and extend great opportunities for growth. I really enjoyed the Poetry on Demand experience. It gave me so much joy to hear each poet write in detail about me as a person. I will hold that memory in my heart forever. You are a safe, healing space for us all. Thank you for being you. Love ya girl.

AJ Wone

Your contribution to the poetry community is much needed. You are a poetry powerhouse that could stand alone but you always find time to give encouragement and inclusion to many. I appreciate and respect the person that you are and how you are very giving when sharing resources that are viatl to helping the growth of individual artists. Continue to be a positive light and welcoming spirit to all. Much respect.

Hiram Sims

I want to express my sincere gratitude to you for the opportunity to get my words out on paper. From day one, I felt welcomed, I enjoyed every class and looked forward to attending each week until the pandemic happened. You created a way for students to continue to work on their craft which was amazing. Even though I have connected with so many great people, I have learned a great deal about different forms of writing. And I'll forever appreciate how you helped me learn the history of poetry which was something that I never knew before I joined the group. You make each class innovative and assist in helping students develop their craft. I also appreciate the encouragement and the participation in class play which I thoroughly enjoyed; I thank you again for all the wonderful work you have done and wish you all the best in your future endeavors.

Table of Contents

Acknowledgments xi

Preface xix

Dope Poet.. 3

Connections 4

Between... 6

US 7

Tantalizing... 9

Elucidate 10

Seduction... 12

Chocolate Lips 13

Craving... 14

Panties 16

Captivating 17

I do not love you as if.. 18

Devastatingly beautiful... 20

Music to my mind 22

Colors... 23

Not Looking... 24

Honey Kissed Lips 25

He/She is.. 26

Her kisses drive him wild 28

No building four walls 29

Belonging 30

Restricted 32

Feels Good 34

Honestly 35

Soul Love 37

Partly the Blame...40

Lost inspiration 42

Formula 43

True Confession 44

That forever 45

Into you 46

Being 47

Fight or Flight..48

I still miss you...50

Mistreated 51

Amazing 52

Lonely 53

Silent Language...55

Plug me in 56

I want to be loved Uncompromised...57

Precipitating Factors..58

Ride 59

No, it's all on me 60

Orchid 62

Beautiful Eyes...64

After the Pain..65

The great pretender..66

Don't..67

The eclectic symmetry 69

Consumed with regret 71

Love Remains..73

This Guy...74

Pressure 75

Sorry...76

Lost in translation 77

Over 78

Sorta Kinda 80

Dissertation of Exploration 81

Butterflies 82

Healing 83

Trauma bond 84

Eyes Wide Shut 85

Views 87

Journey 88

Broken pieces of a shattered heart 90

Vibrant 92

Travel with me 93

Accidentally on purpose 94

Unsure 95

Not Looking 96

Lay with you 97

Her love starts slow 98

By design 99

Comfortable with me 101

Destruction 102

Free 103

Discovery 104

We made it 105

Levitating above water 106

Gift 107

Mind over matter 108

Weak 109

Preface

I have discovered that too many people do not believe in themselves and are lacking self-love and acceptance. The goal of this book is to reintroduce you to yourself, and the beauty of self-love. This book teaches the importance of self-love, teamwork, and respect. Discovering self-love is a great life-changing experience.

From over 20 years of experience, teaching, holding workshops for groups, and studying how to love, I believe deeply in the educative value of interpretive discussion of self-love for all, especially in today's society. I also believe that self-love could be learned at any stage of your life, and you can enrich and strengthen others by teaching and leading the discussions and practices presented in this book. Participating in interpretive discussions can help not only yourself but also others to learn to use their minds, and hearts to start the quest for self-love.

There are many different interpretations of love; it's important however to find the correct and efficient ways to love. Self-love should be natural, but for most, this could be difficult to do. When you start to love yourself first, you will see positive change in every aspect of your life. I have been teaching young people for the last fifteen years and many of my students actively helped to shape my understanding of love and influenced my teaching, and I wish to thank them.

Connections
between us

Dope Poet

There is power in the tips of your fingertips
Your manuscript could heal a soul
with a familiar tone your voice speaks
relatable truths that are birthed from within you

We need more of the lessons you learned
to stop a Tragedy form manifesting
your words could be the key to adjust
Releasing your truth

The day has arrived it's time
The book releases the birth of your words
for all to witness this event hand clapping
finger snaps loud yesssssss girl you did that

Praise dance and jazz music playing set the mood
mellow vibes good times food for the soul
smiles on the faces of everyone in the crowd
The overwhelming feeling of gratefulness, gratitude, love, & support

Everyone that was invited showed up
this is so dope I'll never forget this moment
My words are encrypted in the pages of the book
that I created Locked on computer screens
one click purchase read by the minds
of the ones that needed this

I am living in a dream my community is lit
thank you, Hiram CLI we did this,
I needed this
Started in season seven
TA in season eight
alumni season 10 finish we all win

Thank you to the ones that believed and helped me succeed

Connections

Our lips collide and with every breath
it ignites my soul
travels through my bones
I am addicted to the sound of your voice
that breathes oxygen into my lungs

fixated on the touch of your fingertips
that pierce my soul caresses the interior
of my heart your words rhythmically
gives me life like blood that flows through my veins

My body flutters each
and every time I reminisce
of the first time in between time
which brings us to the now

Speak life into Me
Value my role
Grateful tears
Spiritual connection

we are one
I close my eyes
I can touch the moon
and see the sun behind

wait wait

Ok right there
I feel you deep inside me
the piercing of my body with respect
and in return I'll reciprocate

trust, love, and loyalty,
enter me deeper
stop don't let go
allow me to hold your heart
this is a sensational feeling

hands intertwined
your body and mind
keep your mind open
to dreams of the close to perfect mate
feel me up with the warmth of your touch

Hold me tight don't ever let go
penetrate my mouth with truth
taste the nectar of my thoughts
heart fueled with joy
enjoying you

Between

Caught between
standing for what's right
or what's right now
wanting to be a part of the in crowd
setting all morals aside
and choosing sides

Losing friends
just to fit in at any cost
sold your soul for a maybe
or what could be
playing the part of a flunky

Standing between
what's wrong or right
Invisible lines

US

They labeled us
Branded us
Abused us
Owned us
Used us
Turned us
Separated us
Mistreated us

In my lifetime I have never been mistreated disrespected
turned-on abused used cursed put down
led astray by no one other than my own race

I never knew what hate felt like
the betrayal the envy the jealousy
the disregard the lies the backstabbing
the mistrusts the misleading and it all came from us

I was taught that they were the bad ones
they were the racist ones
they were the ones that were disregarding me
put me down, lie on me, backstab me, betray me

I'm not saying that they're not some racist out there
that don't like me, but I've never been in a situation
where I had to face fears in front of them
it's always been us

The nightmare walking
psychopaths talking
the predators the rapist the
child molesters my mother my father
my sister my coworkers us
my own race
were the people that look like me turned on me

Disregarded me raped me beat me
betrayed me lied on me gave up on me
but never have I ever given up on us
I still love us fight for us stand up for us
I'm the just one amongst us
that's going to change the stigma about us in our community
All it takes is just one of us to change
how we think and feel about us
how we love us how we connect with us
how we treat us how we care for us how we are there for us

how we show up for us how we build with us
how we value us how we are loyal to us
it is time for us to change us control the narrative
no more nightmares
no more fears no more tears build trust in us

Us

Tantalizing

A great piece of art in human form
strong broad shoulders tall dark and handsome
the sparkle in your eyes captures the intense
piercing of your loving soul

he is beautifully woven together
a masterpiece
his heart is the connection to his thoughts
he leads with love in control of his emotions

he thinks rationally with other's feelings in mind
logically responds to continue the peace in his home
a strong man bold in his stance
willing to take a chance on love again

one who never gives up
a true believer in a strong family bond
great provider
an example set for the men that follow him

believer in self creating generational wealth
he is swain for the women that he chose to hold his heart
he continues to build his family with love as his solid foundation
creating a safe place to be heard

feel secure without judgment,
he appreciates equality
he values life and the opinions of others
supporting dreams setting realistic goals

teaching truth a protector
snap shots of success
Blessed
A believer in The Most High
My desire

Tantalizing

Elucidate

Tunneling my vision
while our life was spiraling out of control
words lost in translation
our lines were crossed up
in misunderstood words

There were plenty of explanations given
when he found out she cheated
it didn't make sense
unreasonable expectations of what life should be

but in actuality her life didn't include me
had me questioning if I was enough
did I listen did I care
I was really there
there enough to see her pain

supporting her dreams
taking care of our family.
I was wrapped up in my career
never noticed the tears the fear and pain
in her eyes her heart turned cold

Betrayal

She wasn't honest with her feelings
she played games I can't read minds
this isn't the first time
I've held on to what I believe was meant to be
for better or worse to death

I didn't sign up for this
she wants me to provide spend time
forgive her lies give her grace
forget all of her mistakes

I'm paying the price for being a provider
if I was there more, he wouldn't be a factor
she needed to be held kiss touched
feel like a woman so she did what was best for her
late night text the phone rings once and she hangs up

It's no surprise that the child isn't mine
but I'm the only father he knows
she says DNA doesn't make you a father
you're a coward if you walk away
my heart and mind are disconnected
I reject her orchestrated words

I could have forgiven her if there was only one
but to my surprise there were plenty
and still no father for her son

Elucidate

Seduction

Intoxicating aroma fills the room
candles lit set the mood
Slow jazz playing slow tunes

I laid across the bed
Legs spread
Back arched

He laid on top
Touched my spot
Moisture overflowing

Consummating our union
He enters me deep
Pleasurable moans

His kisses dances on my flesh
His hands travel across my breast
I look deep into his eyes

I pull him close
Wet his lips
Our tongues dance
Beautiful climax

Seduction

Chocolate Lips

I long to taste your chocolate lips
I watch them closely
every time we're together
I close my eyes

imagine you inside
my lips touching yours
what a great feeling
chills run up and down my spine

when our lips collide...
I enjoy your chocolate flavored kisses.

Craving

Middle of the night craving
Dreaming of our last encounter
Wanting you right now
She closed her eyes
Reminiscing

She sets the mood
They're both in tune
Eyes locked

She removes the damp towel
From around his waist
Kisses his face

She grips his side
Slide down to her knees
Fulfilling his needs

He moans with pleasure
She plants passionate kisses all over him
As he lays down, she caresses him

Her body wants his
He pulls her close
She crawls on top

He's aching to be inside her
She begins to ride him
He flips her over

Gripping her flesh
Spreading her legs
Pulling her close

He penetrates her deep
She can still taste him on her tongue
She kisses his neck
He goes deeper
Explode

They are both satisfied completely

Panties

I'm in the mood
Take me
Claim me

panties removed
His mouth between my thighs
His fingers inside

His hands are warm
I close my eyes
His tongue is deep inside

Pleasurable moans
Take your time
He grips my thighs

Looks deep in my eyes
Pin my arms above my head
Enter me deep

Slow rotation
Left and right
Up and down

He kisses me softly
She tingles with excitement
Here reminiscing

Captivating

With you is everywhere
I want to be –

Slow passionate tongue kisses –
half-naked cuddling

Pull me closer
deep eye connections

Caress me from head to toe
taste me and after tasting me
he realized he'd been starving

I do not love you as if...

I do not love you as if
we just started courting
wanting to learn more about you
excited when my phone rings
and your name appears across my screen

answering your call
mesmerized by the sound of your voice
ending the 2-hour call
you hang up no you hang up 1, 2, 3 you hang up

I do not love you so if
you were my first long lasting passionate French kiss
from the timid girl that was very adventurous & curious
wanting to explore her sexual side
in love with the desire to be your prey

I'm not in love with you as if
your long stroke penetrated my insides
when I misconstrued love for lust

I do not love you as if
I screamed your name from pleasure or pain
imagining this is what heaven feels like
and wanting to explore more the next day

I do not love you as if
I would take a second chance
on our relationship
and rekindle the magic
that I imagined our love to be

I do not love you as if
we took that last trip that ended us
because you weren't man enough
to explain the reasons why
you didn't want our child and left me in pain
physically and mentally to decide
fighting to learn the reason why

I do not love you as if
I love me passionately and deeply
to walk away
from an eternal love
that will never be
because of uncertainty

Devastatingly beautiful

He stood six feet
three inches
broad shoulders
dark chocolate skin

Perfect eyebrows
his lips honey kissed
medium built
deep sensual voice
when he spoke it made me moist

In depth conversations
relating
sharing dreams
team

He is a well sculptured
piece of art in human form
Chiseled chest
biceps
six pack intact

He is the epitome
of black full lips
wide nose
Strong a place called home

I continue to reminisce
images of you
laying here next to me

I hear your voice
feel your touch
your sensual
luscious lips
collide with mine

When I close my eyes
I feel you beside me
I can almost smell you
taste you
I want to escape into you
I want your hands all over me

My tongue massages your neck
and relieves all of your aches
and stress
I fall asleep
thinking of you
you fall into my dreams

I awake with you still on my mind
wanting to feel you
in between my thighs
I am craving
to be tasted by your tongue

Come home

Music to my mind

Intimacy is more than
just the physical interaction
it's the music you hear
when you're in his presence

the overwhelming of happiness
vibrations on high
engrave your sweet nothings
on my flesh

press deep into my veins
where your words of love
will remain
please let's start graciously
each day

to relive our happiness
each and every day
breath e life into me
ignite my heartbeat

oh how your words
of great encouragement
hit the spot I crave you
each and every day

you're such an enticing thought
nothing more attractive
than a man that helps you grow
and you pour into one another
for growth peacefully, healthy in love

Colors

Color lines
MLK had a dream that one day
we could be treated equally
A dream deferred

We continue to fight for equality
March for what should be right
We are our own worst enemy
We are divided even when we are united

Color blind
It's not a black or white issue
It's an us issue

Division: divided we stand
divided we fall
You could never be me
I could never be you

End the hate within our race
Stop trying to outdo
Outshine
Compare

Color Lines
Light skin
Brown skin
Dark skin

Colors should never divide us
Education should never define us
Money should never control us

Let's celebrate each other
Win together
We are powerful united
Undivided

Not Looking

Heartbroken, excruciating pain
she gave her all to him and them
The love wasn't reciprocated;
they all gave into temptation

She had relationship trauma
believing that there were no good men
until she met him.

She believes in the myth that all men ain't ish
Watching the women in her life get played
That would never be me she proclaims

Her first relationship high school sweetheart
he cheated with the cheerleader

Her second relationship freshman in college
he cheated with his professor

Third relationship a preacher
he cheated with the Dickens wife

Fourth relationship that's going really great
he proposed they got married
he cheated with his work wife

She decided to give up on love
it was too much for her heart to bear

She decided to pour into herself
get to know who she was, live life for her

She hasn't given up on love
knowing that she has to heal
and true love will indeed find her

Not looking

Honey Kissed Lips

His gentleness
makes her weak
And his dominance
makes her wet

He cupped her face
In the palm of his hand
Pulls her close
Wraps his lips around hers

His tongue penetrates her throat
Her body begins to lose elasticity
She falls into the soft silk sheets

He entered her slowly
She reacted with indignation
When he stopped in mid stroke

What a tease
He knows this makes her quiver
With excitement
Of what's next to come

He covers her in honey kisses
Lands in her favorite place
Igniting with fire
His mouth is magical

Her toes curled
He finds ultimate pleasure
In satisfying her
His honey kissed lips
Drives her wild

He/She is

He is fine
he's a catch

She is a dime
she is blessed

We look beyond the exterior

It's his mind for me
the heart you see
transitioning into
who you are destined to be

It's her drive for me
The commitment you see
taking care of business winning at all costs a boss

He is not easily angered never gives in to temptation

She controls her emotions and is aware of her tone

He is emotionally available not codependent on her for growth

She listens to understand and doesn't place blame

His love isn't based on what she could do for him sexually

Her love isn't based on what he can do for her financially

His kisses drive her wild it's like fire when he comes around

He starts with foreplay
gently rubs his fingers
up and down her breast
place his hand gently on her thigh

massages her from head to toe
he caresses her face straddles her
He wets his lips
and passionately kisses her forehead

each side of her cheek
her chin her nose
He licks his lips
and plants them directly on her

He inserts his tongue inside of her mouth
and begin to suck her tongue
moves his head in a circular motion
his pants begin to bulge

He plants kisses on her neck
Shoulders and breasts
He undresses her from the waist down
begins to kiss her below her waist
she moans with pleasure

moves down to her stomach
around to her belly button
makes his way down to her inner thighs
Inserts his tongue
passion overflows

Her kisses drives him wild

She starts with foreplay
gently rubs her fingers
up and down his chest

places her hand gently on his biceps
massages him from head to toe
She caresses his face straddles him

She wets her lips
and passionately kisses
his forehead

each side of his cheek
his chin his nose
she licks her lips
and plants them directly on his

She plants kisses on his neck
moves down to his shoulder blades
around to his chest
makes her way down to his stomach

She undresses him from the waist down
and begins to kiss him below his waist
he moans with pleasure

No building four walls

Things are not suffice
I hold peace, comfort and love
I am home
A vessel
where you can take solace

No judgment
Fighting is out of the question
Communication is relevant
Holding one another accountable

Truth is welcomed
in every prospective

I am home
Love is the house
You have the key

Open up your heart
You'll see
I am more than love

In me you'll find
Peace
Joy
Understanding
Trust
Loyalty is a must

Belonging

I belong to you and you to me
I've been longing for this love
For a lifetime you see

It's overdue
You mean the world to me
You know it's true
It's always you

I belong to you and you to me
I've been longing for this love
For eternity

I'm grateful to experience this
true undeniable love
honored that we chose to take this journey
together you're more than worthy
of this love we share
nothing else can or will ever compare

I belong to you and you to me
I've been longing for this love
for a lifetime you see

Your touch warm embrace
I can see the love all over your face
the sweet nectar of your kiss is something
that I could never resist

I belong to you and you to me
I've been longing for this love
for eternity

We've been on this journey
searching for a love like no other
rewriting our story
you & me no in between
undeniable love destiny

Belonging

Restricted

The eclectic symmetry of the ocean waves
clear skies great times it was all a blur
lifeless body heart stops no pulse
drowned my life in fear

I was buried my whole life
conflicted restricted out of touch
the feeling that I was missing so much
rhythmically contractile
consisting of 100 beats per minute

Able to reproduce times two
bringing in new life
while I'm watching mine flash by
my mind is racing I'm praying
but no one hears me

I feel submerged by the clumps of dirt
that's placed on top of my lifeless body
this can't be the end
I have so many unfinished things
the light is calling me

But I don't want to go
there're so many untold stories
and I can't let go
I'm trying to hold on
and be strong to the end

conflicted restricted out of touch
the feelings that I was missing so much
I need I need you I need you
please don't allow this to be the end
it's not the time for my demise

I feel my fingertips tingling
I'm still alive my eyes pop open
but I cannot move
I cannot breathe
I hear somebody saying it's time

I hear the click clacks
the rolling of the chains
lowering down my body in a grave
people chanting
from ashes-to-ashes dust to dust

We lay our loved one to rest
no, she did her best
I live my life without fear or regret
But this is not the time for me to be at rest

Restricted

Feels Good

I feel good about this
This friendship our relationship
I needed this
Someone like you to turn my gray skies blue

Someone who seems to understand
some of the things I went through
it's easy to open up to you
I know you pay attention I listen

You're a strong man that's taken plenty of changes in life
You have made a conscious choice to do right
I know it's hard, but you've made it this far
times will get hard

but just know I'm here for you whatever you go through
whenever you need me to
I'm always here for you
I enjoy all our time we spend together

it's such a pleasure
you are so amazing though my eyes
you're a treasure.
I know things will get better

In time we will see if you and I are meant to be.
I'll always be true I love you

Feels Good

Honestly

I wasn't my true self these last few months
I was lost and consumed
with doubts and fears
of the what ifs and maybes.

Not believing that we could be more
holding on to resentment
not allowing time to heal me
mend what once broke me believing
that we couldn't get that old thing back

I was afraid of giving all of me entirely
to you and not reciprocating the same in return
I was lost and confused
making irrational decisions statements
my mind was racing

I was afraid of losing myself in you once again
my guard was up high
I messed up big time simmering in my bitterness
my heart and mind on different wavelengths

I wasn't in a good space
no excuse
I don't want to lose you
not again this can't—shouldn't
please don't allow this to end
give us a fighting chance

I know I messed up big time man
my heart is hurting
head in an unfamiliar space
please don't take your love away
I know you need space but wait

I've been without you for way too long
I know you're tired of hearing this same ole song
allow me to show you that it could be
what we once had before

I don't want to lose you once more
you hold a special place in my heart
that no other has ever compared

Our souls are intertwined
yours and mine
a deep connection
more happy times are here to share
I'm lost in despair I truly care

This love is rare
truth meant to last forever
honestly, I don't want to lose you again
my real life-long friend

Honestly

Soul Love

My soul searched for the one that was lost
misplaced taken away my soul ached for you
stayed up late thinking of who what I should do
how does a lonely soul get over you stop thinking?
wishing dreaming of reconnecting with you?

Your soul moved along moved on
settled for what may be wrong
yet you're still hanging on to what wasn't meant to be
I gave up but couldn't shake you reached out to you
wanting to reconnect my soul is aching please yes yes yes

Detached from what I thought was meant to be
but one day I received a rude awakening
no explanation time passed me by it seemed like eternity
my soul was mismatched detached living a lie
began to turn cold I thought we'd grow old guess I was so wrong

Don't walk away love my soul is hurting love
this wasn't a mistake love you chose wrong love
but now you're gone love how did this happen love
this can't be real love

I settled on being alone
because in my heart no one could ever
replace what was real not for any reason
not even a season
true love could never be threatened
but life teaches us many lessons

If I ever fall in love what?
I did and now my soul continues to ache
for you wait up late for you
dream realistic dreams of you
wishing it could be with you,
but I know it will never be the way it used to be
no more just you and me

My soul will always love your soul
but never depend on you to be whole
or complete but still yearns for you
hoping to get over you but never giving up on you
but can't stop thinking of you never wanting to lose you
but being real.... and will it end still? come on keep it real

I'm afraid of replaying the thought in my mind
of being connected to your soul again
but it's like I never lost you my friend
real love is what I found in you
and you in me my soul isn't complete

I need want to have NOT just a piece of you
but all of you create new memories with you
build with you stay up late with you
plan with you live out dreams with you
win with you happy with you trust

No more pride allowing my soul to hide
I've allowed the pain to subside
no more passing me by
no more pretending like I'm alright
without my soul love don't move along love
I've found you again my soul love
no more hiding love

This is the end love my real love ...you ..
no other love you have my soul love
I'm content love no more pretend love
your soul complements my soul love
let's stop dreaming love and make this official love
you make my heart smile love

A connection so deep I feel you in my sleep
anticipating the day that we reconnect souls
connected no questions together again
like it never ended no need for questions
explanations I'm at peace with you my true soul
lover and friend—
The Lover of my Soul

Soul Love

Partly the Blame...

I've been here contemplating on how to tell you the truth
behind all this hurt and pain and yes, you're partly the blame.
I've been hurt too many times to fall back into that trap
babe I want you all the time please come back
we were the perfect match.

all we need is us forget the others
having me just depending on you
man, what you put me through
all the hurt and pain and lies
the other girls you had on the side,
but you only want me to remember all the happy times.

Plenty of time has gone by
as you can see.
I'm a woman now only depending on me.
man stop trying to sell me a dream
I live in reality

I know you know what I mean
I'm not that little girl that I use to be
when you controlled me
I lived for you now I've moved on
to bigger and better things.
now let's' talk about our past relationship

When you tried to break me down
man, you were a trip listen to this tip...
there are no second chances
we've been down that road
and I don't want to go back
yes, I still have LOVE for you really, I do,
but I'm not in LOVE with you

I'm telling you the honest truth.
So please move on
because this boat is sailing along
I know you want me back, but
I can't help you with that
I don't feel the same and you're Partly the Blame...

Partly the Blame...

Lost inspiration

He was my muse we were so in tune
beautifully intertwined
mind body soul and spirit humbling experience
just the thought of you brought out
magic with my pin
passion love life truth

I wrote a whole book just about you and I
all the amazing time we spent lived imagined together
the warm existence we experienced
it can't be completely explained
but you get the picture

Photographic memories
I traveled many miles just to be in your presence
I awakened each day happy as can be
you were my peace my confidant
and most importantly my friend
the love and support were endless

Until one day it ended
shattered dreams misplaced souls
stories began to unfold
happiness began to fade
no more happy home
tears shed misconceptions
twisted words explosive confessions

I lost you
distraught confused
no longer my muse

Lost inspiration

Formula

Equation
my life is parallel to the line Y
equals four minus one
how do I function without the 2
what does it mean to be functional?

passing through the Y
how can I determine what's your line?
as it relates to my life
when I came from disfunction
and now I pay the price

I sit back and examine
trying to find the answers
to change the Y is the question
sometimes you might find the answer
but history cannot continue to repeat itself

so, I have to find a formula
for the four that I helped to create
so, they won't have to continue to ask the question Y

I may not ever get the answer to the problem
that I'm seeking no matter how well I graph out my life
and re-create the number line until I get it right
I will continue to try divide, multiply, subtract
Until my life is on track

Formula

True Confessions

I was never in love with you
I was in love with the idea of you
a figment of my imagination
you were never true

An unrealistic desire
that I created in my mind
of what I imagined you to be
then I awaken to the tragedy
a tragedy of you

who you really are?
a narcissistic serial liar
that plays on women's kindness
a fool with no soul

A half man
who would never be whole
were anywhere his home
a creature of habit

Who lives lies
for the entire world to see
posting a life that's full of fakes
He's green with envy

full of rage
he can't deceive me
my eyes are open

I see the truth
the feelings that I had
Will never be again

it's sad because
I was one loyal
friend it's the end
no more
I'm not a woman scorn

True Confessions

That forever

Some say you only get
that once in a lifetime kind of love
that rare love
don't want to share love
that real love

that I got your back love
loyal love...
never ending love
no upgrading type of love

until something shakes up love
you try to erase love
but can't forget love
no mistake love

that find its way back kind of love
I'm here to stay forever love
no matter what it takes love
priority love

can't allow it to dissipate love
attempting to repair
it's real love
I'm all yours love...

love is like a game of chess
you make the right moves to protect
your queen and in turn she protects her king...
A team type of love—

That forever

My Love

Into you

I'm into every inch of you
I love everything you do.
when we're alone together
I'm mesmerized

when I look deep within your eyes
I feel you
I feel a deep connection with you.
It's much more than just sexual

it's also intellectual
you're my water to my fire
my calm to the storm
my next chapter yes, I want more

My never-ending story always a happy ending.
you're my sunset at night
oh, I love it when you hold me tight
all the late-night conversations

Getting to know you has been a blessing...
In my life I've learned many lessons...
and it hasn't yet crossed my mind to let you go
there's so much more I want to know
I'm digging you fo sho

Into you

Being

Your being has a purpose
at first you don't get it right
you search yourself
try to find wealth
and accomplish many things in life

But still you haven't found you
your existence
your purpose
What's the focus?
Why do you exist?

What's the reason for this???
Who is ultimately responsible for your existence?
How long does it take to find who Am I?
Again, what is my purpose for this life?
your being is intriguing

Our being is an instantaneous flash of light
in the mist of eternal night
Was it just coincidental that we met?
Was it by chance?
Or do you believe in fate?

Whatever the reason
I'm astonished that we found one another...
I'm intrigued by you
Turned on by the things you do
In time we will share an exploding experience

it's going to be so pleasurable
allow me to paint the picture
Naked bodies dripping wet
this will be a night you'll never forget

Being

Fight or Flight

Subconsciously I analyzed the situation
looking for the truth
hard to find it's what I already knew
processing all the million bits of information
that I stored away in the past
everything coming full circle
I really hoped it would last

In my heart I knew it was a situation
I possibly couldn't get through
all the signs were there
but it was like I didn't even care
fear started to settle in the threat was there

Thinking back to the mornings afternoons nights
that we shared processing the memories
and if you truly cared
looking for anything to compare
looking for recognizable patterns of deceit

The threat was detected
stress kicked in again should I stay,
or should I go I freeze overwhelmed
with the thought of being alone,
so, I overreact runaway instead of
facing the issue head on
he responds inappropriately
and says irrelevant things to the matter at hand

Anxiety kicks in I sit still
calm down so we both can be heard
and respond appropriately
still debating should I stay or should I go
What's the risk to face the chance?
of a bad consequence

The level of risk was on me
this was our second time around
no different I see still caught up
in the same position prior to the reconciliation
but I made the conscious
decision to overlook all the signs
my fault this time

The severity of risk for this outcome
to depart was high
I failed this time, but you didn't even try
all feelings die the pain too much
what you gave was not enough
you pushed me away
but still contemplating on if I should stay

Fight or Flight

I still miss you

I can't separate my feelings
no matter what I try I thought it will be forever
until we die, I can't believe it's over
for real this time I replay the end over and over in my mind

I'm happy on the outside sad sometimes
but all in all, I still miss you at times my
heart races when you cross my mind
I know the love is real but still it's no more you and I

It was time for us to end
thought we could still remain friends
but you decided otherwise
not in my plans it was time to let go
move on carry on let go
of the memories dreams good and bad times in between

I still miss you I still miss you
I don't know what to do
to relieve this pain
I'm still sane trust the process
disconnect no regrets
put it to rest walk away with my head held high
knowing I at least tried
but there isn't a day that goes by that you do not cross my mind

I still miss you

Mistreated

Great Deception

He held her with high regard
but treated her like a used car
one on a used car lot that everyone passed by
without a second look
No regard for her feelings

took her out on dates
treated her like a queen
posed for pictures together
but posted the selfies of only him
of every trip but she wasn't in any of them
memories on his timeline
of just him no them or they

He came home every night
Excited about life
Made future plans
Reassured his love over and over again
Even introduced her to family and friends

His life came crashing down
The day she came back in town
And reunited him with his child
Reality hit now both of us our
Face to face believing we each were
The only one it's over I'm done

Amazing

I just want to sit here in silence and admire
the man that sits before me
take in all his truth he's amazing yes you
my king one day soon... we will ride this wave of life
weather whatever.

fly high together you & I...
so deeply connected our hearts will beat as one ...
our love will reach the moon and kiss the sun...
blissfully in love ...

oh, look at what we've done...
walking in purpose
learning, teaching, uplifting, standing as one...

our souls are intertwined yours and mine.
mastering this beautifully sculptured being
freeing me of these myths that men ant ish...
I'm amazed by you I believe you're the truth...

When you speak, I listen to every word inhaling all of you...
an amazing being, father, son, brother, serviceman, and friend.
a stand-up guy... the most high has blessed you with joy within...
and now he has given you a gift a new best friend...

With time we will blossom and find love within, travel the world...
stand side by side through good and bad times...
overlook one another's flaws mange it all, and if everything else fails...
love will prevail overall...
standing ovation applause...

patiently waiting anticipating for the day, we meet....
our souls will speak a connection so deep I feel you in my sleep...

Amazingly together as one...
I want a better view... you...

Amazing

Lonely

I'm in a place an empty space but I'm not alone
 want to feel at home...
unsettled misplaced overwhelmed
feelings unparalleled confused domed...
our relationship seemed great from the start
we were never apart after a while you started to depart...

I questioned the space was this relationship a waste?
at times my heart felt heavy
I knew something was left unsaid
a secret buried deep I found out the truth
and said my speech no peace of mind
I said I was fine, but questions still lingered in my head
I want answers the truth so I can bury them dead...

Confusion delusions when I close my eyes
I imagine things I can see beyond your well thought out words
refusing to accept the explanations that was given
I'm getting fed up this relationship is a mess distress...

You can't always have who or want you want I guess
I'm not his first choice...listen to my voice
in my opinion It shouldn't be this hard
I shouldn't have let down my guard
so now it's hard to let go exhale oh NO...

I'm tired of being the only one trying to make an effort
his so-called love comes with strings people pulling him every which way
and that's why I can't stay it's time to walk away...
I need someone that is in charge of his life not being confused
of, what's wrong or what's right...

Sometimes opening up your eyes is the most
painful thing that has to be done
I despise people who lie or try to sell me a dream...
I don't know why we are here restless nights I need peace I can't sleep.

Many things have been questionable throughout this relationship
too much reading between the lines...
Situations bad vibes ill feelings lonely times
I don't want to be anyone's last choice...
I've been that plenty of times before
and I don't want to open that door once more...

You know how I feel I always keep it real.
I have a lot to offer love, loyalty, trust, respect that's a must
and someone one day will see it and appreciate me
and what I bring you know what I mean...

But it's no hard feelings I truly understand
your family, and friends come first—
I wasn't a part of your plan I now know where I stand.
It's not a big fuss... this departure is a must.
At this age I'm only interested in consistency, stability, respect, and loyalty...

A foundation something leading to forever a courtship
not just a fly by night relationship people are a trip.
Honor respect and love honey I'm home sweet words
romantic getaways walks in the park after dark
planning for forever when will we start...

At the end of the day yes of course I want to stay,
but if I do, I'll remain in this empty space
I never dreamed of someone taking your place
I loved you from the start you were my heart...

But somewhere along the way
you decided that you needed space
which left me in this lonely place...

Lonely

Silent Language

Silence is a language of its own
to hear my silence
you must know me
on a different level

you cannot research this language
it's untold
it's felt through the soul
scattered words can't replace

the silent language
which communicates
by smiling eyes
a head nod

fist bump
a warm touch
a hand shake
or a warm embrace
that says
I love you so much
with intensity in your eyes

Plug me in

I'll be your socket enter my walls Y
our name I will call all night long...
plug me into you the pleasure you'll feel
when you do...electricity flowing through...

Temperature raising oh the sensation
sparks flying my walls are about to explode...
use your tools patch me up drill into my walls
insert your scroll.

Excitement anticipation currents running through...
electrifying thrilling oh what a feeling...
Plug me in

I want to be loved Uncompromised

If the question was asked, could he
would he
my answer would be NO
and I would have bet my life on it.

Without a doubt I trusted wholeheartedly
but if I would have taken that bet, I would have lost it all.
well, I lost my self-respect
I'm broken down torn into millions of pieces

Hurt beyond recognition confused
but it's on me I knew the truth
deep down he really didn't love me

I was just a pound in his twisted game
a web of deceit, lies it cost me my heart torn in half
glass empty shattered memories of the pass that was full of promises

I fall to my knees and ask why?
what did I to deserve this?
excruciating pain I need reassurance that I'm not the blame
I want to be needed to be loved but not by you
when I think of you all I see is blues

I want to be loved Uncompromised

Precipitating Factors

The fact is his behavior always changed
when there was a mention of her name
internal I could not mask the pain external rage

How does one control feelings of outrage?
disappointment heartache just the discussion
of what is what was and possibly what could be brings shame

It wasn't visible to the naked eye
he painted a picture of happiness
which didn't match his actions that was overlooked

Emotional roller coaster fear anxiety stress hit all at once
my head is spinning heart racing time ticking
flashes of the past happy and sad

Was it real? is it real?
time wasted feelings change fear settles in
holding back tears heart races

it seems as though your entire world has ended
everything is moving slow heart heavy
Indescribable pain. Let go move on

Time is ticking let go

Precipitating Factors

Ride

Come take a ride with me
you drive get inside put down the top
feel the breeze a slow ride come inside

make it safe no mistakes
put the joystick on cruise control
hold on tight no rush we have all night

Now I'm ready to ride

Slow jams playing at a mellow tune
what a great feeling good mood
in and out up and down back and forth
so much passion I have to shout

let down my guard now you're
back in control
speed it up
it begins to rain pleasure

I forgot all the pain
we both explode
new memories unfold

Ride

No, it's all on me

It's me not you
I put you on a pedestal
A make-believe version that wasn't true

I created an unrealistic persona
of what I imagined you to be
now I've awakened from my dream
or should I say nightmare

I was blinded by all the good times that we created
overlooked the signs because of the fear of losing
what I envisioned we shared

I was what you considered to be a side
even though we resided together
your mail was addressed to my address
we awaken together attended family events

But I was one of plenty
I still can't fathom how you made the time
to make us all feel like we were the one
funny when I set back and think of all the signs that I ignored

Do you remember the time you called and said you'll be late?
when you actually were on a date
I saw the post on her page you would think I would've been in a rage
the pain of knowing you've been deceitful

It's sad how I thought to make it right and fight
for a relationship that ended before it even began,
I tried because I was wholeheartedly your friend

I once was lost but now I'm found I had to realize it wasn't me
and move forward and just let it be I had to choose me
I couldn't allow you to break me into shattered pieces
I couldn't fathom the thought of being caught up in all of your games

The lies you told but you feel like I was the one to blame
I saw the signs but didn't read between the lines even though I knew
that none of this was true I was caught up in me
not realizing that you were being you the whole time

Reminiscing of all the times that we were together,
but she made phone calls that lasted quite a while,
I was preoccupied with other things and just allowed you to be you
not questioning any of the things that you do
but that was my fault trying not to be a nag yeah that's my bad

After it was all said and done you tried to have me believe that I was the cause
for your mistakes tried to damage me all because I was emotionally invested
in what I thought we had but again it's on me I saw the signs and continued
to stay instead of walking away

No, it's all on me

Orchid

The purest form of love
We search all our lives
We dig deep and look to others for
validation acceptance consideration

We search we hurt we cry
and sometimes destroy
Love at its purest form

When we find what we're searching for
it's like something unimaginable
something that's always been there
deep down inside of us
some of us find it early
some of us search our entire life

Love starts with family
a diverse population of people
some whom we never really get close to
we all bloom in many different ways
depending on how we were loved.

It starts with watering our spirits
our souls knowing that just with us
we are whole complete with just one heartbeat

Bright light direct sunlight
environmental conditions impact our vision
on love we must see past the heartache
and pain that we connect to love.

knowing that as humans we make mistakes
sometimes unintentionally
others by choice listen we all have a voice
the real love has always been inside of you
We plant the seed of truth
our soil needs to be properly nurtured
you have to plant the seed of hope
water the soil of your soul
and root yourself in love.

Orchid

Beautiful Eyes

Look deep inside where you find truth
You can learn many things
by looking into a person's heart, a love spark

Those beautiful eyes speak without words
Captures your soul an eternal hold
look beyond the exterior you'll see perfection a real connection

Those beautiful eyes where you find yourself
Embrace the five stages of emotions most important acceptance

Beautiful eyes hold no lies
close to perfection the connection
the greatest introduction to your truth

Those beautiful eyes see all the beauty you hold within
the photographic picture off extreme joy peace love
and ultimately happiness
all of these things you'll see by looking through me

Beautiful Eyes

After the Pain

I never imagined allowing anyone into my heart
because before I knew what love was it fell apart
I couldn't imagine that anyone could love me more
than I do but I gave it a chance I took a chance on you

I can't say it was all your fault
I saw the signs before it all fell apart
the love was there the love we shared was
is real and true that's why I fell for you
you understood me and I understood you
flaws and all without judgment

It's hard to completely let go
I know I have to move on no more—new beautiful times
I died a little inside waterfalls of tears shed.
body aching with pain when we decided to officially end

I held it together until you walked away
I couldn't fathom the pain if I continued to stay
our lives we are going in different directions
we grew apart I stared out the window
for what seemed like an eternity imagining you
walking back in and will start all over again

I had to grieve you no longer need you
picked myself up and wiped away the tears
got back to me realizing that when you
understand that love starts within
in time I will understand why it had to end

After the Pain

The great pretender

I left before it ended
memories replay in my mind all the good times
we had to stop pretending
notice the different inconsistencies
no sweet names you're all the same at times
I will no longer complain

I sat up many nights continuously contemplating
should I continue to fight to keep this love alive
man, you know I've tried I'm tired of the back and forth
we are no longer meant to be

I wish you well/ we're far away from me thinking about
what we could've been replaying over and over again
the love we shared could it be repaired our dreams shifted

He appeared to be all in
discussions of lifelong plans
confessing his love
making all kinds of plans alone
not considering my feelings
just wanted what was best for him
it's a mess

The love I imagined we shared has all faded away
even though he's here
I miss him what I thought was him
it's all different no more us

He painted a good picture of himself
it was all a lie as time went by
many things unfolded
never underestimate anyone's ability to pretend
to be present in the relationship
I changed my perception
he changed his direction

The great pretender

Don't

A new way to love part one
I will be the right one for the one I was meant to love

I am full of light

With each new beginning comes a great new story.

A story that songs are written for.

Imagine that you found love in me
Let's embark on this journey

Remove all doubts
exhale all of your fears

Hold me close

Let me in to share all of me with all of you
understand that fear is a normal response to the unknown

Allow me to walk in your presence in peace
learn how to just be free

Free from the idea that we have to love traditionally

Traditional is controlled confusion

Confusion creates chaos

Chaos is a form of trauma

Never allow your dreams to be shattered
by the trauma that you sustained

Trauma will not fit into our rules

We create our own rules just me and you

Imagine living a life without fear without control

Just loving naturally open to new beautiful beginnings

You can go your entire life believing that you will never find me

But here I am standing in front of you
the love that you've yearned for

Don't allow me to walk away

Embrace change hold me close don't ever let go

Don't

The eclectic symmetry

of the ocean waves clear skies great times it was all a blur

I was buried my whole life
conflicted restricted out of touch
the feeling that I was missing so much
rhythmically contractile consisting of 100 beats per minute

Able to reproduce times two
bringing in new life
while I'm watching mine flash by
my mind is racing I'm praying
but no one hears me

I feel submerged by the clumps of dirt
that's placed on top of me
this can't be the end
I have so many unfinished things
the light is calling me

but I don't want to go
there are so many untold stories
and I can't let go
I'm trying to hold on
and be strong to the end

Conflicted restricted out of touch
the feelings that I was missing so much
I need I need you I need you
please don't allow this to be the end
it's not the time for my demise

I feel my fingertips tingling
I'm still alive my eyes pop open
but I cannot move
I cannot breathe
I hear somebody saying it's time

I hear the click clacks
the rolling of the chains
lowering down my body in a grave
people chanting
from ashes-to-ashes dust to dust

We lay our loved one to rest
no, she did her best
I live my life without fear or regret
but this is not the time for me to be at rest

The eclectic symmetry

Consumed with regret

heart broken
headache
tired of crying inside I'm dying
I can't face him just yet
give me time space
I need a healing place

Consumed with regret
wish I could take back the words
go back in time and make it all fine
back to the days when he was all mine
I assumed it was time to speak how I feel
but it wasn't the right way
it should have been face to face
my heart feels heavy no time to waste

Consumed with regret
he wasn't ready to hear it yet
time will tell if it gets better
I'll just send him a letter
to explain in detail
why it had to end
but yes, we can still be friends
let me think this through
I believe I still want you

Consumed with regret
I can't believe it's over yet
what do I do should I call?
should I reach out to him
tell him again that I was wrong
can we still try this again?
I miss my friend
I wasn't really ready for this to end
not this way
I'll swallow my pride
try again tomorrow
no more sorrow

Consumed with regret
I'm not ready yet
this can't be the end
I can't lose my friend
his not responding to my calls
my text yet
I hope he will

Consumed with regret
I'll let him heal
but is it the end?
I can't this isn't real
he's ignoring my calls
that's nothing new
all in his feelings
over the truth

Consumed with regret

Love Remains

I'll travel to the end of the world with you
because my love is true no matter how far apart,
my heart still beats for only you

I couldn't imagine going on without your voice to carry on...
our love is like a song traveling in time a great melody still alive
unforgettable never replaceable still standing...

Like a well put together sculpture that will always
be amazing to view oh my god you
I can't help but to stop and stare
and admire all the time we shared you cared

We're like the same but different you paid attention
you listened you had my back and I yours
how could I not adore I'm grateful forever more?

You were real from the start
that's how you captured my heart
one that will never depart but our love is in park

We stayed up sleepless nights trying to get it right—
I don't expect many things from others
it holds no value to me
I don't know them they don't know me

But no matter what our love remains

Love remains

This Guy

I met this guy
he was really easy on the eyes
and kind of fly
he was also intelligent
oh you think that's irrelevant

Oh, you think that I should focus on his manhood
or what's in his pockets
but that's not me I look deeper
do you have a degree?

What was your study of choice?
have you traveled outside of these streets?
I want to know about you before I allow you to explore me
how about you
speak the truth what do you do
what are your plans for me and you?

This Guy

Pressure

Perpendicular force
a stress reliever
close in proximity
ignited with fire
fluids circulating
ready to explode

I've been waiting
temperature rising
combustion releasing reaction
hot enough to warm a room
visibly proportioned
extremely attractive
in tune with each and every inch of you

The strength and vitality sustain physically
power deprived
mentally stimulated
parallel at the right angles to vertical
aligned at each and every level

Pressure applied your body and mind
satisfied each and every way
powerful drive
gentle to the touch

Reset and release
break free
it flowed right through me
breathe
come up for air
no one can compare

Pressure

Sorry

I'm sorry I hurt you
that wasn't in the plan
I didn't give myself time to really heal
mixed emotions steady coasting
reliving memories of the past

Wishing why it couldn't last
or even go back to the way that it used to be
a time and place please let it be
I can't continue to make mistakes or excuses
it's not fair to you or me to continue down this path of misery

We were once destined to be
but now I see no more you and me
you need time to heal
so do I sit here and contemplate
decisions between you & I

Good ones better
ones in between
I should've spoken up at times
I'll let the pain come out
as resentment

That was never the plan
all I wanted was to
remain back in that time and space
where we were one on the same page

Sorry

Lost in translation

Giving too much too soon
I lost myself in you
thinking we were it

I can't believe this is it
you and me forever
but you had different plans

Never gave our love a chance
even though we were together
we were traveling down different paths

Speaking two different languages
you viewed the world much different
not too much in common

You had it all mapped out
what was your life about?
we're never on the same road
I was lost in you

Not realizing it wasn't me
Never meant to be
no more you and me

Lost in translation

Over

Confusion delusions
when I close my eyes,
I imagine things I can see
beyond your well thought out words
refusing to accept the explanation that was given
I'm getting fed up with this relationship is a mess distress...

You can't always have who or what you want
I guess I'm not his first choice...
listen to my voice in my opinion
It shouldn't be this hard
I shouldn't have let down my guard
so now it's hard to let go, exhale oh NO...

Sometimes opening up your eyes
is the most painful thing that has to be done
I despise people who lie or try to sell me a dream
I don't know why we are here restless nights
I need peace. I can't sleep.
Many things have been questionable
throughout this relationship
too much reading between the lines.

Situations bad vibes ill feelings lonely times
I don't want to be anyone's last choice...
I've been that plenty of times before and
I don't want to open that door once more...
I know how I feel. I always keep it real.

I have a lot to offer love, loyalty, trust, respect
that's a must and someone one day
will see it and appreciate me and
what I bring you know what I mean...

But it's no hard feelings I truly understand
your family, and friends come first—
I wasn't a part of your plan
I now know where I stand...

It's not a big fuss... this departure is a must...
At this age I'm only interested in consistency,
stability, respect, and loyalty...
A foundation something leading to forever
a courtship not just a fly by night relationship
people are a trip. Honor respect and love honey
I'm home sweet words romantic get always walks
in the park after dark planning for forever when will we start...

At the end of the day yes of course
I want to stay, but if I do, I'll remain
in this empty space I never dreamed of
someone taking your place
I loved you from the start you were my heart...

But somewhere along the way
you decided that you needed space
which left me in this lonely place...

Over

Sorta Kinda

He was sorta kinda wrong
I was sorta kinda right now

I'm sitting here singing this same old tired ass song
where did I go wrong?
thinking believing hoping and praying
that he was the one listening to my friends

Girl give him a chance let him in so eventually
I gave in wasted two years of my time,
but it was a lesson there somewhere

I convinced myself to settle even to the point that I could help
in the effort to mold him into a better representation of himself
not realizing that he himself was lost and not willing to transform
to reach his full potential of the man he could and should be
but at the end this wasn't working for me not where I want to be
I need out... questioning love

I was making a statement but not feeling love
I uttered the word but when I spoke, I choked
I can't continue to pretend
I'm not feeling it this charade has to end
false representation of self this is too much to endure
my heart must stay pure I can't become bitter
because of this façade contemplating on how to end this

Without being a little shady putting myself first
remembering my worth
just the uttering of the words
I love you to him made me cringe

Can't be fake had to walk away fake love
I couldn't make love I had to wake love no mistake love
or just in case the love fell away love is this some mistake love
and that's not me I have to be true to my soul take control love

Sorta. Kinda.

Dissertation of Exploration

This dissertation is written to explore
my aspersions and expectations of this courtship
not to be too invasive

I just want to inquire and admire
this wonderful being that stands before me
you are my desire nothing like the priors

You're unique in every essence of the word
oooo let me stop and take a breath
and continue this my turn to drop this next verse
better yet take a break and send you a sweet text

Just thinking of you lately that's all I seem to do
can't get you off my mind can't wait to see you next time

Let me get back on track
I want to know all about you
what you plan to do what your future holds
how you set your goals

Sitting here reminiscing of the past
my experiences would this be the one
that last can't focus on the past

Time for new yes me and you
I'm opening up can't shake these feelings
no reading between the lines my punctuation is fine...

Butterflies

I don't know about you but for me
when I first meet someone it's kinda awkward
getting to know them the initial first date wondering
if he's going to eat off my plate

it was always the same place dinner and a movie
and if the date went well the beach for a walk
we talk about things that we have in common
sometimes we get into our goals if he gets that deep

We contemplate if we're going to give him
a kiss good night but maybe not on the first date
a hug should suffice not sure if I wanted to learn more
but I'll wait till he calls to shoot his shot and ask me for a second try

For some reason I wasn't really into dating
I was more into my education learning always
trying to make money I'm on a mission to get
out my horrible life conditions

But on the next date and the next one and the next
I felt butterflies he was my type of guy very
intellectual attentive he paid attention

I thought to myself I could possibly
fit home in my life plans give him a chance

Butterflies

Healing

I decided to stop the cycle
I decided to not allow anyone to put labels on me
to project who they are on to me
I decided to hold my head up high

Believe that whatever I dream I could achieve
healing is a long hard process
it helps put your mind heart and soul at rest
peace is what I seek when I dream it's nothing but great things

It's hard to change who you are
people expect you to go with the flow
move like they move listen to their rules f
ollow their lead but that just doesn't fit me

It's my time to be free waking up keeping my dignity
change in what I see
looking forward no going back
life is beginning to be great

Healing it's a wise decision to make
it's a commitment to change
It's liberating it's free I found my peace

Healing

Trauma bond

It is important to realize when it's time to walk away
it could be difficult sometimes because you can relate
to what another person is going through

You might feel like it's your responsibility to stay
you have to take care of you your heart your time use it wisely

Don't misconstrue love with trauma
sometimes it mirrors the same
I'm here for you I understand you
I love you because we have experienced the same trauma

in life you find yourself in a miserable situation
it becomes toxic
yelling
fussing and fighting
not talking for days
sharing the same space

You think that a hug or kiss or a half apology is ok
don't heal properly you continue to go around and around in circles
making excuses for not only your behavior
for their behavior until it spirals out of control
heal first love yourself first walk away do it today

Trauma bond

Eyes Wide Shut

Blindly building on trust us, but to my surprise I wasn't the only one
tunnel vision overpowered by lust or just the idea of your touch

Late night early mornings phone calls to 1 in the morning
beautiful discussions making plans holding hands
future seemed so bright until that one night
the phone rings but it's not who I wanted it to be
shattered dreams of us our plans
it was you and me but now it's 3

When she speaks, she tells me that she's pregnant with your seed
now it's you plus 2 where does that leave me?
hurt and confused no one to talk to
how could I not see? When I first met you
you were a single man

Now you're a plus 1 carry the 2 you had a daughter
and she has a son my first reaction was to run,
but you apologized and led me to believe that
you wanted me we were good for a while until
I found pictures of you and her plus 1 and the other 1
posing like you're a happy blended family

Oh, what pain I wished death on her name
I haven't heard from you in 3 days
the phone rings now you're trying to explain
this is way too much for my soul to bare
how can it be repaired images going through?
my mind still pictures of you and her or the worst

I refuse to live a lie oh how I despise
how you led me to believe that I was the only one
while you were out playing like you were a family with her
I'm tired of playing games I'm a queen not a spade
I gave you space never once complained
I see the world differently than most people
I believe in truth in whatever you do
a man is nothing without his word

I guess you didn't get the memo, but I hope you've learned
all my thoughts of you use to be good
now they're filled with sorrow and pain

I misunderstood your lies and games
left my heart in pain
you played a good game
now you want me to believe you've changed
and forget all the pain give us another chance
you'll be a better man you just lost the best thing
that ever happen to you fool

I was blinded by you now my eyes are open
wide not shut like before
I can see pass all your games and lies

My eyes are WIDE OPEN NOT SHUT LIKE BEFORE...

Views

My eyes viewed you differently that day you kiss my lips
for the very first time I felt chills down my spine
it was a surprise when your lips met mine

Physical connection the next time oh me oh my
the first time you walked through my door
and you begin to explore me kissing caressing
undressing clothes on the floor

it was a great experience yes, I want more
chemistry begin to form before we were done
I know I wanted more I couldn't keep my composure
physical bliss can't get enough of your touch your lips
is the key to this explosive timeless priceless impeccable kiss

Views

Journey

We were first introduced back in 1992
you were my muse I was intrigued by every vision of you—
It ended before it began, we started over and over
until it seemed perfect, I poured in all of me
until I created what I thought would be
the perfect version of what I needed it to be

I altered you to conform you into what I needed
again and again, I got frustrated at times and quit
believed that would be the end but I just couldn't give up
so, I tried and tried again
and again, until I felt like it was perfected

But I continue to criticize myself I thought this is not gonna work
so, I searched for something that I thought would give me peace of mind
other things, but I always seem to come back to you
you made me happy I think this time I'm gonna stick with you
used as a tool I evacuated to my safe place I found solace in you
I've gotten too comfortable here not something that I'm accustomed to

For years I wasn't able to trust that just me was enough
so, I dibbled and dibbled here and there, but I also found myself
going back so here I am again starting over
yet again this time I'm committed focused
I'm taking notes studying pouring into this
yes, for real 100 percent

Believing in my truth mask off knowing that the most High
will guide me through this challenging time faith is so DeVine
I can't believe that I ever doubted me I'm ready to start from scratch
I connected back with my very first love
it's refreshing pure joy I'm optimistic about the future
the worry and fear has dissipated I'm starting over
giving it my best setting the mode with my favorite tune

You make me happy this I can tell I really love you
Frankie Beverly and maze I start my routine placing everything
exactly where it's needed all my ingredients are in place oh, I can't wait
your taste the aroma the succulent texture all the spices fresh vegetables
food I'm blessed to create it's innate

Journey

Broken pieces of a shattered heart

Broken pieces of a shattered heart
sitting in the corner
glass swept up
by the pail of men
that left them behind
oh no but I'm fine

I told him I wasn't ready
I continued to cancel dates
show up late I'll play this game

She hasn't had a chance to heal
jumping in and out of relationships
before she got over the next
the last one or the one before

Why? She doesn't like being alone
she needs to be held loved
jumping from bodies to bodies is her new sport

People deal with relationships differently
some abandon relationships all together
but for her she loves her peace
and search for love anyway she can get it
some people are afraid of being alone

She stops and thinks of what a healthy relationship
could be could have been trying to find you in them
I guess now, I'm locked up in this cage
my freedom taken away still full of rage
sorry I didn't get to say my farewell or goodbye

I know your mother was hurt that wasn't a good thing
you didn't have any children but so sad no one to carry on your legacy
to be completely honest I tried it wasn't love
it was the chase for me I wanted to win

Sad just a game there was no end
I didn't plan this once you decided to leave for good
I saw it in your eyes this time I couldn't lose you again n
ot to her I don't know what came over me
everything went black when I snapped
out of it I was in handcuffs I heard sirens

Welp, I guess I did win in the end
you played your game and I played mine

Who is the blame?
I blamed you for all the others before
the ones that tore me in half
you were a good man I couldn't see
past the pain your life is now destroyed
now you are at rest

I awaken from my sleep
I never gave him my number
just a thought of going through the pain no rest
all I heard was these beautiful lies before he even spoke
looking into his beautiful eyes

Vibrant

She emerges words from her fingertips
She is the picture of poetry
It lives inside of her like fluorescent
musical notes of an orchestra of sorts

Her energy is contagious
Her light brightens the darkest room
She is so in tune with her emotions
Heart, mind, body and soul

Every mood shapes the voice
She spits fire with every word
that flows from her tongue
it's a ripple effect the beating drum

Her words hit hard the sweetest melody
every song one voice a harp player
twiddling the strings one by one a beautiful tune
Vibrant thing

Travel with me

I have traveled this life
attempting to discover who I am
was and could be

Thinking back on the pain of my past
that has led me to the now

and what I've decided to hold on to
and let go of

unpack
release the hold
move along to the present
the now rebirth
passion is found

Come travel with me to unpack
this whirlwind of pain laughter joy
what I overcame

Accidentally on purpose

Accidentally I fell for you on purpose I loved you
Accidentally I liked you on purpose I'm excited
Accidentally I found you on purpose I kept you around
and it continues...

Unsure

The connection was
Or was it?
The signs were there
But I didn't care

I was caught up in the game
I cause my heart so much pain
No regrets
Did I learn?
Yes

My heart is still open
To a greater love unspoken
Love is still an option
I'm not broken

I want to build a solid foundation
With my equal
I'm here open
There is no sequel

Continue this path of life and love
Through the lens that we see fit
Communication is the key

Trusting loving respecting loyalty
It's not only on me
I'm open for what's real
Not for what's right now
Just my type I want to build

Not Looking

She awakened in pain dried up blood on her upper lip
It took what seemed like hours to pick herself up off the floor.
She began to crawl towards the bathroom
grabbed the door handle for support
stood up walked to the mirror
and didn't recognize herself
her face was black and blue
covered in dried blood

Head pounding migraine she ran bath water
and sat in the tub until the water was cold
too ashamed to ask for help
tears fell from her face
that's when she remembered she was raped
flashbacks of how it started

Blaming herself she contemplated suicide
reached for the razor and began to slit her wrist
believing that no one would miss her so no one would care

Random thoughts went through her mind
No one who believe he did this to me
I don't matter
I wanted it
I deserved it
I should've been at his home at 3am
I knew what would happen

He raped me and took me home
I have to be more careful
It's my fault
It's in me

Lay with you

Intermittently wrapped in the comfort of you
the warmth of your voice sensually whispering I love you

Your words travels through my soul
body on fire my heart is racing

I turn to face you looking deep in your eyes
I see you more clearly
I believe you

Beautiful reflection
I see me inside of you
removing the layers
letting down all Guards

Receiving all of you
no more cold lonely nights
day ends is by far the best as I lay with you

Her love starts slow

Second guessing the unknown
Unfamiliar kisses that curl toes
Ignited fingertips that start flames

It doesn't change when she is in control
she presses her back side against his spine
He turns to hold her

The connection so divine
Soft sensual back of the neck kisses
him gripping her backside

Pulling her close
Tongue Twirls on the back of his neck
Undressing clothes on the floor

Staring in each other's eyes
imagining oh what a prize

She is on cloud nine
He moves in a circular motion
He caresses her with passion

She arches her back and moves to his rhythm
The passion is contagious

Overwhelming pleasure love overflowing
The passion ongoing

By design

Easily disposed of
No value
Used
Abused
Tossed to the side

Playing dress up
6 inch heels
Short dress
Revealing all of you

All To do it over again the next day
And the next—and the next—and the next

How do you sell a human life and sleep well at night?

Her entire life she was told you're beautiful
any man would be happy to have you
she was molded to be a servant

To rely on looks and use her body as a shared cost

Early in life her mother and aunts taught her to
plan to be a bride before she even could drive
living in a fantasy world worshiping materialistic things

She was taught to be polite
always hold your head up high with grace
make him notice you
be the baddest in the room

What a mistake

Her Life shouldn't be easily disposed of
Manipulated into thinking that you could put a price tag on her
Her mother died in an abandoned apartment building on the East side

Her aunt was hung in a crack house
Her family structure crumbled
She never really knew her father
but was shipped off to him because he was next of kin

The system felt it was best to be reconnected with family

She had to pick up her life and move to an unfamiliar city

She took a two-hour plane ride with a stranger
who told her everything is going to be alright
this is what's best for you

The stranger introduced her to her estranged father and brothers

The first time she was raped she was 12
By her older brother

She told her father after she was raped again by her other brother
Her dad smiled and said now you're ready

She felt she had no choice
She put on the attire that was given to her by her mother
six inch stiletto heels a short spandex dress face full of make-up
and headed out to work the streets

This went on for what seemed like forever

No one asked her name, her age

One day she got tried and refused to work
They found her body burned in the middle of a parking lot late at night

Selling her a dream of what a beautiful life could be cost her her life

That's what the system would do

Comfortable with me

I enjoy my alone time
I'm also a social butterfly
I set boundaries never crossed the line
I'm a giver of time
I don't enjoy the shine
I'm destined to be great
Make no mistake I enjoy my space

Destruction

Explosive reactive
unsettled in this place
out of place
picking up the pieces of my pass
release take a seat exhale

When all else fails put on a face
no time to waste
attempting to discover who I am
what I want to be
searching writing out my past

Life has been a whirlwind
no proper guidance
loss no love, no trust
who I am ?I'm terrified of becoming a failure
not amount to anything or overcompensate

So many failed friendships, relationships, family ship
I found myself changing jobs
each time I felt conflict not facing it head on
time to move alone
holding everything inside

Headache, heartache, excruciating pain
stuck in my own guilt
not living in the present moment
struggling with my past
searching for the truth
in the deep dark corners of my mind
I need you this time

Free

My mind is free of fears
No more pain, tears, afraid of the unknown
I'm free and prepared to move on
There is nothing holding me back
My future is awaiting I am on track

Building a foundation of great accomplishments
My team is ready in full force
Class is in session
Poetry flows through our souls
Writing out a vision just watch all the stories unfold

Free to be what I was destined to be
A writer, creator, boss, author, mentor, teacher, business owner
the sky is the limit

Watch us win—when one wins, we all win

Discovery

Understanding the purpose was hard
 but hey you got this far
You need to know what this change will bring
don't become a prisoner of your past
overcome no more overlooking be the priority

They never just let you be great
so find greatness in you
spread the love and put joy into everything you do
discover you at a time when you were lost
and brought yourself back to life without a cost

living out your dreams
living free to be who you are
you've been through so much
if I sat down with you for a while
I will continue to ask how

It's time for you to walk in your truth,
bury the past and discover who you really are

I hope your today is so much better than yesterday...

We made it

A warm safe place to be
welcoming
you feed my soul daily
your passion for your work
shows how much you love each and everyone

No one is ever left out
heart overflowing with joy
Attention to detail caring giving inspiring
knowledgeable you show up and support

Always there when it counts
a blessing in human form
when I think of where I'd be
if I didn't believe in me,
it's truth when you speak

Positive vibes all the time
I thank the Most High for you
he came through standing ovations
this is my dedication no one can compare

Living out your dreams and still working
with your team no one left behind
we all gone shine watch one another
grow one step at a time

Loyal to the very end
I love you my friend
Above influence a teacher and a student

Levitating above water

Struggling to breathe

It's hard to see

My heart is racing
Self-Revelation
It used to hurt to hope

Levitating above water
Shallow breaths
Hard to breathe
Life flashes

No future in sight
In and out of consciousness
untangling the dysfunctional
layers of my life

Hard to move
Beatings worse
Black and blue
Internal pain

I'm going insane
Spent my life running
To survive

Hiding in the shadows
of my pain
Time to
Let go move on
breathe

Gift

The innate capability to originate
the rhythm of trumpets playing
the beat drops from the drummer

rhyme begins to flow
Piano Keys flaring
a magical sound blaring
beautiful musical tunes

the spotlight shines
it's our time so divine
we write the verses
that brings the vibes

you feel the rhythm
which births the rhyme
grooving to the sound
we all shine so divine.

Mind over matter

The human brain is powerful
Believe it is and so it will be
Manifest positivity

You're loved
You're appreciated
You're extraordinary
You're valuable
You're wealthy

Body, Mind, & Spirit is powerful beyond measure...

Weak

Being a victim of self
living in the mindset
you'll never get well.
Hi, my name is victim

It continues to be a mystery
to me how could you despise
or hate me
when you don't even know me
when you look like me

We face the same struggles
share similar backgrounds
your assumptions block reality
You stand in your own way
teaching hate due to your insecurities
who hurt you? it wasn't me.

You are a victim of circumstance
molded by the lies you were taught
By the weak ones you follow lost

About the Poet/Writer/Chef

Andrea Lee is a multi-talented poet, chef, and author known for books such as *The Power to Change the Way to Love Yourself*, *Connections Between Us* and the upcoming *Expressions of Love, Feelings of Love, Courage & Betrayal*. In addition to her adult-oriented work, Andrea is also venturing into the world of children's book writing. Her passion lies in helping others understand the positive connections they can foster with one another.

Her works have been featured in various publications, including *Stunning Poetry* (Silent Spark Press), *Poems in Praise of Libraries* (Sims Library of Poetry), and *1619 Speaks* (CLI Books). As the founder of www.writingjourney101.com, Andrea has developed platforms like Poetry in Motion, a literacy programs for teenagers and young adults, and Writing Journey 101 Press.

As a host of a weekly poetry show on Let's Talk Radio, The Artist Connection, Andrea connects with her audience every Thursday at 8 pm PT. Born and raised in Los Angeles, she is a proud mother of four children and dedicated to empowering her community.

Andrea is an alumn of the Community Literature Initiative, where she continues to be involved as a Teacher's Assistant. Andrea is a member of Poets in School with Los Angeles Poets Society. Her poetry has been showcased at various venues, such as Inner Health Care Ink and Holy Grounds Cafe, reflecting her commitment to sharing her passion for writing and fostering connections with others.

www.ingramcontent.com/pod-product-compliance
Lightning Source LLC
Chambersburg PA
CBHW051320120626
46547CB00015B/2320